Éditions DIASPORAS NOIRES

www.diasporas-noires.com

©Emmanuel Ngombet 2019

ISBN digital version : 9791091999939
ISBN printed version : 9791091999946
Date of digital publication : May 25, 2019

Legal Notices

Emmanuel NGOMBET

The desirable future of Humanity AFRICA

A part of a STRATEGY for the NEAR FUTURE

Essay

English Translate   by Jenny GAUMBERT
Colorado city, Colorado, USA
&
Boris BAMVI
Dakar Sénegal

Foreword

The great lesson that we learned from the present migration to Europe, is the globalization of causes and effects, which leads to new concepts such as:

Moral ecology

Social economic interference or type of social, global and united, governance of the world

Digital territoriality

A necessary interdependence of the countries' economies
Interdependent economic intelligence beside economic war

The weapons of war or 'thin cows that eat the fat cows', in the Pharaoh's dream, interpreted by Joseph

Preface

My attention was drawn by successfully explaining, step by step, in the simple words a concept as difficult as the global social govnernance of the world.

My attention was drawn by successfully explaining, step by step, in simple words a concept as difficult as the global social governance of the world.

In our political environment (a totalitarian regime dominant), the risk taken to explain and propose a drafting of governance acts (expression of the interest, terms of reference, is high.

The pedantic boldness, in the statement of innovative projects (the production and transport of freshwater from the sea to the arid lands of the interior of Africa), and structures (the increase in production of electrical energy (15 GW), and/or, refining all our minerals, locally on the continent) leaves us enthusiastic !

The subject seems very technically to me, but in this changing world where knowledge is one of the most shared thing, through digital technology, let us take this opportunity in order to help the African populations to embrace the vision of the free trade Africa

Free trade forces the decision-maker to surpass himself (become a citizen) and to govern differently (continental and planetary human vision)

Arsène Francoeur NGANGA
Teacher Research in Historical Sciences
And Co-founder of the NAICCE

Introduction

A suggestion of a collective strategy for the African continent, Alvin TOFFLER says
"If you don't have a strategy, you are part of someone else's strategy."

We propose a ranking, a list of priorities for optimum results with a domino effect, because time and favorable circumstances are also to be apprehended.

The construction of the barrage (on the Nile) by Ethiopia (economic necessity) will seriously reduce the quantities (flows) of the water on which all of Egypt depends. The freshwater project for all Africa can provide a sustainable solution and prevent us from having a water war between countries.

We are declining, for Africa, the offer to acquire nuclear power plants for electricity production because of the danger that it represents, the high implementation cost, the obligation of a social organization of labor and the level of awareness (individual and collective) that our countries have not yet reached.
The basic need of Africa is the production of the freshwater, by desalination of seawater, and the transport of that water

to the arid lands of the interior of continent. The presence of water on those areas makes it possible to plant large quantities of fruit trees and vegetables to ward off famine and food dependence to imports

Africa's energy potential allows for the production of clean, abundant, renewable and cheap electricity
The permanent availability of electricity will open the possibility of REFINE locally on the continent, all minerals, including and in particular crude oil, to obtain the lowest cost of chemical derivatives and petroleum products, such as JET A1 which conditions air fares

Immediately and without delay, Africa will take the shortcut to the use of electric cars and trains, new information and communication technology

In GOD we stand – In GOD, we remain ! This will be the motto of the continent, where men, thanks to planetary citizenship, induced by the globalized ecology of the FREE SEATING – FREE MOVING – free TRADING will become earthlings, simply, living together (notwithstanding the variation in melanin pigmentation rate) in the cradle and the desirable future of Humanity : 'Africa'

Part I of the strategy

Freshwater for Africa from G5 SAHEL to G55 AFRICA SWEETWATER, 55 000 men or 1 000 per country, 94 billion Euros.

The project plans to withdraw one million m^3 from seawater everyday from each site through five units of 200 000 m^3 each. An annual consumption of 3.365 m3 of seawater which gives a quantitative assessment of the environmental impact on the ocean Atlantic and Indian

Through a system of pipe and water towers, freshwater will be transported from the sea to the arid lands of the interior of Africa

The project expects the creation of private freshwater management companies delivered by WATER PURCHASE AGREEMENT, to guarantee the repayment of the loan and the quality of the product.

A related project, the production of fruits and vegetables will begin with planting large quantities of fruit trees and vegetables in all irrigated areas made cultivable by the presence of freshwater. Africa would therefore produce the quantities of food necessary for the continent's food safety and a significant reduction of food imports

Recommendation 1:

Creation of G55 AFRICA FRESHWATER : 55 000 men or 1 000 per country

A €94 billion loan over a 50 year period from China, through the privileged partnership with Africa

A general mobilization for freshwater
A single project to lift Africa out of famine, poverty, massive food imports and assistance

Part II of the strategy

The second priority is the collection treatment and recycling of urban waste

We are dealing with a public health problem. All you have to do, is to travel through our major cities to see, for yourself consequently it is not unexpected to see the outbreak of cholera or typhoid in Kinshasa or the proliferation of cemetery rats in Brazzaville.

Construction of urban waste treatment plants in all major cities in Africa.
The urban waste tax will be levied on each household or citizen to make this ecological activity profitable, to be managed by young people in companies

Recommendation 2:

The second priority is the collection, treatment and recycling of the urban waste

The creation of jobs by setting up this business of collecting, treating and recycling waste from every city in Africa, a positive profit will be

A push for ecology, at the global level and shared by all

A global citizenship, globalized, through ecology

Part III of the strategy

Production of ecological, abundant and cheap electricity with regard to the continent's energy potential;
Transport and distribution of electricity on the continent

Abnegate and refuse to import nuclear danger into the continent, in order to avoid the proliferation of 'nuclear fire' and its possession in a 'moment of madness' by radicalized people

The permanent availability of electricity everywhere on the continent as one of the conditions for the emergency, in 2025

The African Union, pursuing its objectives of achieving the conditions leading to the emergency of Africa, has adopted as the third condition and priority, the abundant and cheap production of clean and ecological electricity, through :
- the construction of all hydroelectric barrage

- LNG valorization through the construction of gas-fired power plants
- the establishment of renewable energy plants and
- the implementation of the HV / THT grid for the entire continent

Renewable energies, including hydroelectric power, remain the simple and rapid solution for accelerated and harmonious development based on a clean and sustainable energy source 'AD AETERNAM'

The valorization of gas, flared on the platforms and in storage
This project consists of liquefying the gas, currently flushed and in reserve in the basement, storing it in large quantities and then :
- Export. Ports and high – capacity storage areas will be built to facilitate the storage and export of liquefied gas. The studies will also examine possible gas purchase contracts as means of guaranteeing investments
- consuming locally in the continent. The household and industrial gas bottling industries will be set up and the marketing will be formalized. These industries will be sold to private individuals to guarantee the loan but also to help the economic emerge through diversification.

Nuclear energy, in addition to being a very expensive luxury, is a threat to people's lives,   a crime against Africa. The creation of a nuclear power plant (nuclear waste bin),will be, if we are not careful, a serious deliberate negligence of continent's gigantic energy potential.

Nuclear energy requires precision in its maintenance program and a high level of awareness (individual and collective) of the society organization of work, which our countries have not yet achieved.

Recommendation 3:

Africa can claim ecological and renewable electricity (solar, wind, hydroelectricity), according to its huge energy potential.

Europe is dismantling its nuclear power plants and would like to sell them to Africa.

Why would the continent import the danger of the nuclear option, at the very risk of being delivered a nuclear power plant, where the waste of others will be stored, if it has not been sent into space.
- Abundant and cheap power production for all Africa .
- LNG valorization project electricity production (domestic gas) and export
- Pre-export mineral refining project

- Fair for projects power production and transport through Africa

Part IV of the strategy

Refine minerals locally (iron, copper, aluminum, crude oil, etc) on extraction site

The aim is to initialize the ore deposit and the ore processing process on the surrounding sites.

From iron ore to steel locally (Gabon and Congo) could jointly acquire blast furnace, rolling mills and steel mills tore fine 15 to 25 % of the extracted ore on site within five years and reach 50 % on 2025

These industries will include blast furnaces and rolling mills needed to process iron minerals from the Mayoko deposit and steel production.

Zambia wants to increase its production capacity for locally refined copper to 50 %.

The DR Congo will be supported in order to equip itself with the materials and equipment necessary for the transformation of copper at Lubumbashi

Cameroon and Guinea Conakry bauxite, will be by electricity abundant and cheap, refined to 90/95 %

The installation of industries using steel, including any assembly lines (cars, locomotives, wagon, train, etc...)

The project is intended to settle based industries of iron and steel for the local production of all types of equipment and gear from the cheap steel of the Congo and Gabon, and copper from Zambia and RD Congo

The agency space FUNSU N'ZINGA will be the ultimate goal of the steel-based industries, the lowest cost of the world, because of the presence of cheap electricity.
Africa enters the space age.

Part V of the strategy

The knowledge economy, the economy of the health and the economy of the digital technology

The knowledge economy, the economy of the health And the digital economy or the construction of:

- Two to ten university centers by country
- A University Hospital Center and an adjoining Medical Clinic Center to every university center to widen the offer of health and validate the universal health insurance.
- A building, by university center, Sheltering the center of incubation of companies and START - UPs

Recommendation 4:

- Bring the fiber optics in all the African countries
- Cable all the cities of Africa very broadband, 10-100 M/bits
- Attribute scholarships immediately for training (100/country/year for 5 years) to cover the deficits

- Build university centers by country
- Build University Hospital Center and ' Medical Clinic Center ', adjoining university centers to increase the offer of health and validate the universal health insurance

To take into account the urgency and the partnership favored with your country, China will prefinance 5500 scholarships by year for five years (that is 100 scholarships/country/year) in universities of China and in the African universities

2019/2020

- Project Scholarship for training of the young people of all the countries of Africa
- Project construction of university centers by country
- Project exchanges students and researcher

Part VI of the strategy

The electrification of existing railways and the construction of new tracks

The present state

This multi-variant project will make it possible to

- bring the track gauge of the current tracks up to international standards thus allowing the purchase of rolling materials from any manufacturer worldwide
- achieve the electrification of railways by using our energy potential produced by all hydroelectric barrage, gas-fired power plants and others
- build new railways lines, 1 500 km long. From Pointe Noire to Bangui and Kinshasa (via the road / railways bridge of the Congo River at Maloulou).
- the networking of news lines in DR Congo, do not forget to mention the rehabilitation of existing lines

- The layout of the new lines, the construction of the power lines and the stations are the main focus of this project. The new mines are:
- The main purpose of this project is the routing of the new lines, the construction of the electric tracks and the stations. The new lines are:
- North West line, 3600 km ; Kinshasa / Bandundu / Lisala / Gbadolité / Zongo
- North East Line, 4,000 km; Kinshasa / Bokungu / Kisangani, Bonalia, Stopped, Juba
- East Line, 3,500 km ; Kinshasa / Kananga / Kindu / Bukavu / Goma / Kigali

- South Line, 3,500 km ; Kinshasa / Kenge / Kikwi /Tchikapa / Kamina / Lubumbashi
- West Line, 600 km, Kinshasa/ Brazzaville/ Pointe Noire, via the road rail bridge
- South West Line, 1,500 km, Kinshasa/ Luanda

Only in Central Africa the need is 50,000 km of tracks to be built, maybe 100,000 km for all of Africa. An opportunity to ask China to build locomotives/cars on the mainland.

Part VII of the strategy

The single African Sky and the opening of the air transport market in Africa

The construction of the unique sky and the opening of the market of the air transport in Africa
- Serving president of the UA will lead in 2019, the meeting of all the service providers Aviation of the continent, which will end in the agreements on the Project of interconnection and interoperability of all the networks of the ANS PROVIDERS

- The meeting will pronounce on the Project equipment of the secondary aerodromes of all the countries of Africa, to fill once and for all, the holes of cover of flight safety and absorb the absence of skills noticed within the DACs

- The project of a common satellite (for all aeronautical telecommunications) will be discussed and validated to serve as a solid base in the construction of the African unique sky.

through interconnection and interoperability (and even the merger) of the ANS PROVIDERS of the continent.

In Brazzaville, in 2019, serving president, will lead the experts to take forward the opening of the air transport market in Africa on the following projects:
- Project "poles of leasing of planes"
- Project "centers of maintenance of planes, certified"
- Project "modification of the legislation of countries for the validation of the opening of the air transport market"
- Project "fund of financing of the leasing of planes"
- Project "insurances of planes on the continent"

Recommendation 5:

All the ways of transportation are to be implemented with modern concepts:
- In Central Africa, the electrified rail transportation, from the center that establish Brazzaville and Kinshasa, at destination of all the capitals of the zone CEEAC (Luanda, Lusaka, Bujumbura, Kigali, Juba, Bangui, Yaoundé, N'Djamena, Pointe-Noire and Libreville).

A profitability assured by the travel(movement) of the 140 million inhabitants, allowing the refund of the loan
The possibility of asking to China to take up the assembly shops of locomotives / cars on the African continent and help

refine locally the iron of the Gabon and Congo and the copper of the Katanga

- The transport by inland waterway on the river Congo for three concerned countries (RCA, RD Congo and R Congo and by producing in the passage 10 Giga Watts on every bank of the river, with marine turbines put on banks in the not navigable places of the river

- The civil aviation or the economic free trade area has just widened the horizon to the projects such as:

1. The projects of implementation of the African unique sky

Project ' Interconnection and interoperability of networks '
Of all the service providers of aviation in Africa

- ✓ The first step of the unique sky, is to make have a dialogue, at the technical level, all the networks of the various ANS PROVIDERS of the continent.
- ✓ THE ASECNA and ATNS began a common program,to spread to the others (Nigeria, Angola, RD Congo, the Maghreb)

Project equipments of the secondary aerodromes of all the African countries
Project of training and capacity buildings of the staff of the DACs

- ✓ Reduce the holes of flight safety ensuing from the insufficiency of equipments in the secondary aerodromes
- ✓ Train enough the staff of the DACs to decrease the zones of not competence.

Project Satellite aeronautical telecommunications for the African unique(only) sky
Optical fiber project of interconnection of all the airports of the continent

- ✓ A common project, a network of satellite for all the aeronautical telecommunications of the continent
- ✓ The common satellite + the satellite of NIGERIA in backup 1 + the satellite of Angola in backup 2
- ✓ The fiber optics of interconnection of all the airports of the continent in backup 3

FUNSU NZINGA, launching site of rockets or space industry in Africa

- ✓ Extraction of the iron ore and the aluminum from 300 km (Mayoko, Owendo, Mfouati) of the launching site
- ✓ Refining of the iron, the aluminum and the gold, on sites near the deposits(fields) of extraction
- ✓ Electricity production, ecological, plentiful and cheap from 500 km of the launching site, 1200 MW of Kouilou Sounda, 3000 MW of 10 gas plants, 2 GW of INGA III
- ✓ steel based industries

✓ Manufacturing of satellites

TRAINING CENTER OF THE COSMONAUTS in Africa
  ✓ In Chadian Tibesti, Faya Largeau and in SARAYA / Kédougou (Senegal)

2. Projects of the opening of the air transport market in Africa

Optical fiber project of interconnection of all the airports of the continent
  ✓ The exchange of the data of safety and of security,
  ✓ The supply and the installation of the new control X of luggage, with labeling in face recognition of the passenger
  ✓ Project "Navigation by Satellite – GNSS"
  ✓ The navigation by satellite concerns any ways of transportation today
  ✓ Its implementation on the continent had already been acted by the African Union

Project " poles of leasing of planes"

Project "centers of maintenance of planes, certified

Project "fund of financing of the leasing of planes"
Project "insurances of planes on the continent"

- ✓ The market of the plane (leasing, maintenance, insurances, support for the financing)
- ✓ Present strong growth perspectives, in particular in the preservation of the capital gains of the insurances planes in Africa

Project modification of the legislation of countries for the validation of the opening of the air transport market in Africa

Develop a single legislation, by merging the scattered texts of every state, to facilitate and fluidize the air traffic of the continent, by taking place administrative red tapes of the DACs

Construction project of the complementary commercial infrastructures for Maya, the extension of the terminal, the airport village and the airport private hospital of emergencies(urgent matters) for Agostino Néto, the zone air freight, the hydrant, and the private hospital of emergencies(urgent matters) to increase the state-owned receipts of the concession.
The price lists (and rates) of air services, returned by the dealer will have revised downwards to affect the prices 'low cost ' temporary tickets on the continent

Project of refineries in all the countries producer of the crude oil.

- ✓ The price of the fuel stays a high expense brought up in the operating costs of airline companies
- ✓ The producing countries of Africa can supply low cost fuel (-21 %) by arranging refineries

Project absence of visa and unique common passport for African (acted on March 21st, 2018 in Kigali)

Free Moving - Free Seating - Free Trading without visa for the Africans or unique common passport, for all Africa as a condition of free circulation of the people and the properties in the ZLEC

3. Projects of flight simulator in 55 flying clubs of the continent

4. Flying school Project, near the center of maintenance plane

5. Project of the university of the meteorology of the countries of the pond of Congo (private university)

- ✓ The agro meteorology and all the branches of the meteorology Connected to the Space agency in Libreville

6. Air Transport business Project, near the pole of leasing of planes

7. Emergency clinical project of airports and fleet of hospital planes

Part VIII of the strategy

Conservation of the forest ecosystems

Taken globally, the second wealth of the countries of Central Africa (CEEAC) will be the capacity to preserve Ecosystem foresters intact for the future generations.

The purpose is to accept the forest conservation as the wealth of tomorrow

The moose of preservation of the forest, the ecosystems of the pond of Congo and environment is going to bring us to reduce (15 % a year and during five successive years) the cutting of trees. The wood will be less and less taken in bits, until 75 % on the horizon 2025, for the happiness of our traditional pharmacopoeia and for the sake of future generations

For five years, the import of the electric cars / vehicles will be taxed in a fixed price (VAT) of 5 % to encourage the citizens to change their cars / vehicles fossil fuel; by new environment-friendly models and of the climate. Proposals of assembly lines are expected.

Recommendation 6:

Africa can still keep its forest ecosystems and benefit from it in 50 / 100 years

Africa can already and directly switch to electric cars and trains, without waiting to reach critical thresholds of pollution

With the presence of the fresh water in the dry lands of the continent, further to the project G55 Africa fresh water, we can reforest Sahel and end the famine, the war of the water and poverty

AFRICAN UNION

Resolution n° xxxx / 2019 of
(According to the introduction of electric motor cars in Africa in the park automobile national public / private, as a replacement fuel-fired models fossil)

HEADS OF STATE

Considering the Treaty establishing the African Union.
Considering the objectives of the millennium fixed by the NEPAD
Considering the constraints of the fight against pollution by CO_2 emissions
Considering the necessities

DECIDE

First article: with regard to the observed climate change and in the objective to keep(preserve) the forest ecosystems and to reduce the air pollution in our country, import of electric motor cars in Africa, in the park automobile national public and private is encouraged by a preferential customs rate to 5 %, as a replacement fuel-fired models fossil polluting.

Article 2 : All new import of cars and sedans old model fuel-fired fossil, public or deprived, is forbidden as from January 01st, 2020.
An exception will be observed for Machines, Trucks and vehicle of construction site(work).

Article 6 : present resolution, which repeals any previous opposite capacities(measures), will be registered(recorded) and published to the gazette of all the member states

Made in Addis Ababa,

Signed

Serving president of the African Union

Recommendation 7:

New measures of preservation of the maritime ecosystems, the treatment of urban waste to limit the pollution of the ocean

State of the society

The sea in our country, was destroyed and soiled, until 75 % of our reserves.

It was plundered by its fauna up to fries, including in sea bed

The national are marginalized by this activity and the rural fishermen are discouraged because nobody listens to them, especially not the state employees of ministries delivering the permit / licenses of fishing to the foreigners

Impact of the measure

Stop net the plunder of the fishing fauna and the destruction of the maritime ecosystems

Return the masses and the surfaces exploited at 25 % of the current authorizations

Slow down the impacts of climate changes by the observation of a period of three (3) of the ban on the fishing to allow the renewal of the resources

The urgent matters of the climate change

We owe from now on, to watch with the modern ways, the exploitation of the fishing resources of the sea.

The overexploitation and the devastation of the sea puts in danger the survival of the fauna, of it and the flora and even of human races.

The fisshing licence are delivered in the big groups, in particular, Chinese, which exploit in national waters, H24 - J30 and A365 and with explosives (dynamite, pomegranate and very fine nets of stitches, scraping everything, everything!

The quantities of the urban waste poured in rivers, in sea and in river Congo are so enormous, as they transform them, little by little, into swampy trash cans

the implementation of the processing centers of the urban waste of our cities (and consequently production sites of the biogas) is an ecological urgency

AFRICAN UNION

Resolution n° xxxx / 2019
(Concerning the preservation of the forest ecosystems in Africa)
HEADS OF STATE

Considering the Treaty establishing the African Union.
Considering the objectives of the millennium fixed by the NEPAD
Considering the constraints of the fight against pollution by CO_2 emissions
Considering the necessities

DECIDE

First article; with regard to the observed climate change and in the objective of preservation of maritime ecosystems in our country, all the authorizations of fishing in national waters are cancelled

Article 2 : every developer for the sea fishing is subjected to the renewal of his authorization of maritime developer on the following new conditions:
- The reduction in 25 % of the total volume of the grips, formerly authorized

- The reduction in 10 % of surfaces, formerly authorized

Article 3 : every developer in sea fishing is subjected, with the cooperation of the services of the state skills, to proceed to the reduction of the taken species, in the same sites according to the mapping of the grips

Article 4 : any use of explosive (dynamite, pomegranate) is forbidden. The respect for the period of ban on the fishing, for three months every year, is compulsory to guarantee the renewal of the fishing resource

Article 5 : the penalties of breach go to the seizure of the material and the used boats

Article 6 : the state makes obligation, in any built-up area to initialize its plan of waste treatment / garbage domestic until the construction of a sorting office / treatment and recycling

Article 7 : present resolution, which repeals any previous opposite capacities, will be registered and published to the gazette of all the member states

Made in Addis Ababa,
Signed
Serving president of the African Union

The HEADS OF STATE

Part IX of the strategy

The countries of Africa and the weapons of war

The weapons of war or "lean cows that devour fat cows", in the dream of Pharaoh, interpreted by Joseph.

Profits engendered by the economic activity and especially the sale of ores, were gobbled up in the purchase of the weapons of mass destruction which did not serve; The weapons of Gaddafi scattered in the Sahel since his death, for the terrorism

Mines antipersonnel put by SAVIMBI will continue to cut legs

The MIG of the Angolan and Egyptian army is made rusty on the ground, by default of enemy and budgetary restriction.

The new president of ZIMBABWE, newly in the throne, buys weapons in quantity in a country where the unemployment touches the 45 %

President IDRISS DEBY ITNO of the Chad exchanged funds(collections) reserved for the future generations to buy weapons, overcome its opposition and assert itself as a military power within the G5 Sahel. He was not able to solve thorny problem of the drying out (90 %) of the Lake Chad, which engenders the war of the water in the North Nigeria and in the Central Africa Republic

An eyebath of the old scale of values, the power of nations through their destruction capacities

The new humanity which is spirit to be born is the one of:
- The quality of life,
- The reduction of the air pollution
- The collection, the treatment and the recycling of urban waste and especially metals.
- The cleaning of seas, oceans and rivers to avoid transforming them into immense swampy trash cans.
- The reseeding of seas and oceans (and rivers) and forests, by species in overconsumption or endangered.
- The breeding of the fish and the animals is an urgency of food safety
- The production of fresh water (by desalination of sea water) and its transport in dry lands of the inside of Africa is a necessity and a basic need to crash fruit trees and vegetables, in very big quantity,

We have just passed the threshold of natural regeneration of the resources. The culture of the picking, the hunting and the fishing, practiced since the dawn of the humanity, is at its end. We should now grow, recycle, clean and conserve.

Recommendation 8:

Africa remains the continent of the future of the humanity, if his managers abstain from being equipped with weapons of war in very big quantity.

The President Abdel Fatah Al SISSI signed the purchase contract of fighters and diverse security systems. These two billion Euros to be put for the benefit of the factories of desalination of sea water (port Sudan in the Red Sea) and of the transport of the fresh water to the desert of Egypt refilling, the Nile, in small daily doses (on the south border, the monuments of Nubia).

The army will be in charge ' of leading this titanic / Pharaonic task, of bringing the water ' in all the Egyptian desert and to crash fruit trees and vegetables of the prosperity.
The war of the fresh water, with the Sudan and Ethiopia, will be avoided.

The factories of desalination of sea water of Ziguinchor will end the conflict in Casamance (becoming again the attic and the forest of Senegal) and will re-fill to Sikasso, the river NIGER..

President Mnangagwa signed the purchase contract of weapons. These funds would have been able to be profit of the joint contract with Mozambique, the production of fresh water, by desalination of sea water, and its transport in the dry lands of Zimbabwe and Botswana.
The young people in the unemployment (45 %) will find an activity and he can claim to stay in power, without the use of weapons

What ghosts (or devils) haunt the nights of the African leaders (and managers), tilting them on the 'security armament', in front of the choices of food safety of survival of the populations and the development of the economy?

Why choices leading the massive destruction of the human nature, still take him, in a more and more globalized world, where the worst enemies of yesterday (French and German), agree to build together, Europe?

Who wants the peace, does not prepare the war, but contrary to this mental posture of the bottom of ages, gathers the conditions of conservation of the peace, including sharing of the wealth of the planet by a global social governance of the world

Part X of the strategy

The intangibility of the inherited borders and
The part of the endless conflicts

A "touareg" state like the Swiss in the sands of the Sahel

Sahel G5 will reach with the strength and the means involved, long-term ways, to reduce the Islamic terrorism in the zone, but cannot prevent the latent survival from attacks. It is necessary to take into account the existence of the stocks of weapons come from Libya and spread in the hiding places of the desert (from Mauritania to Niger)

A political solution would be desirable.

SOMALIA LAND
In spite of indicators (of peace, development and democracy) more convincing than those of the South Sudan, after their independences, SOMALIA LAND deserves an international recognition of its sovereignty, a kind of MONACO / Luxembourg.

Recommendation 9:

The desert of Sahel was always 'Touareg' since millenniums. The plan of the borders of the independences of the 60s, is a historic anomaly which deprived them of the freedom on the lands.

And why not, a state as the SWISS, without army, for the Touareg of the AZAWAD
Sahel G5, after its results of the war front, will have to change into embryo of the new G55 Africa fresh water.

The G55 Africa fresh water is going to give a visibility of development, clean and long-lasting, through the project production and transport of fresh water (after desalination of sea water) to the dry lands of the inside of Africa, and firstly the lands of Senegal, Mauritania and AZAWAD

The purchasing power of the African is very low in the point where they cannot allow to buy weapons. Weapons used in Africa, however is the conflict, were bought from the budget of a given state. By sleights of hand, they escape their seclusion republican in private caches (opposition and/or majority) where from they are going to sow death and sadness of the civilian populations, the victims innocent of slave traders of a new kind;

Part XI of the strategy

Emergence by space industry

Base launches Madingou Kayes
FUNSU   N'ZINGA

Strategy of Emergence by the Space Industry

- Local, abundant and cheap electricity production
- Refining ores (iron, bauxite, gold, crude oil) as close as possible to the ore extraction site. The lowest costs.
- Manufacture of rockets and satellites; near refining sites
- Launch base, attached (less than 200 km, manufacturing plants
- 5 years of long-duration space flights – 3/6 months, robot-driven, nuclear-powered
- Construction of the training center of the cosmonauts of Faya Largeau (Tibesti).
- 5 years of training and training of our first cosmonauts

Proposed new concepts

The globalization of causes and effects leads to new concepts such as:

Moral ecology:

Take back funds hidden by African leaders in tax heavens and of fact selling their real estate (accumulated in other countries) which are worth more than €1million, and allocating those sums to the SWEET WATER production project, keeping them at 10 % among the shareholders of the infrastructure management companies set up by the said funds, is more has matter of morality than law.

In kind of ecological morality at global level, made possible by the traceability and transparency of financial flows, whatever their nature, amount and destination, to overcome the pair of shortcomings of the current system.
Another form of economic intelligence by preventing and repairing the flaws that cause great poverty.

The concept of economic warfare is giving way to moral ecology, economic justice in solidarity yet economic intelligence, interdependence.

CFAF 5300 billion (but 8 billion euros) in the accounts of six african leaders in Canada. Failure to assist people in danger by squandering their public property by their own leaders. Aiding and abetting and participating in a criminal enterprise that has resulted in economic and financial crimes against a country and people

Economic interference yet global social the governance of the world

The replacement of fossil-fuelled cars by electric cars is a good example of economic interference for reasons of combating air pollution, climate change and poverty. A guarantee is provided by the Ministry of Finances in a (external) bank and/or in the countries concerned; Every time a customer subscribes to the ELECTRIC CAR loan from a local bank, the manufacture and his dealer are paid immediately. The loan (24/36 months, 20 Euros per day, yet 600 Euros per month, 14,400 to 21,600 Euros net) will be recovered by the local bank at a rate not exceeding 10 %, each day through payment in mobile money Airtel money or daily cash payment. Nearly 55,000 electric cars per year throughout tea ZLEC.

To help promote the end of hostilities, the current Chairperson of AU (alone or accompanied by another French or Chinese President), arrives with these solutions, with his counterpart in the form of a transfer of crude oil:

- Robot construction for a program of 50,000 social housing units (with solar tiles) per year in the country
- Airport reconstruction (terminal high rise, technical block, airport hotel with 250 rooms, airport emergency clinic, international conference room, cargo boat area
- Massive introduction of electric cars (2000/year) and multi-source electric bollards (3 to 10 KWH) in Sudan.
- Generalized vaccination and universal health insurance at the expense of the State of Sudan for the next 5 years.
- Rehabilitation of schools with installation of a server and 50 reading lights per classroom using solar energy produced by solar roof tiles

Doing nothing will only make things worse
A kind of <u>social, global and solidarity governance of the world</u>

Digital territoriality

The UNIVERSAL BOX, combination of freebox / livebox and phone THURAYA, will ensure digital territoriality to all.
So whatever my momentary position on the surface of the Earth, a citizen will have access to all services in his home

territory, at about the same cost by adding very low roaming charges.

The international connection to not penalize companies and citizens, in case of national restrictions.
The ordinary BOX will find its place where fiber optic conditions will be met.

A necessary interdependence of economies
Economic war as opposed to interdependent economic intelligence

The weapons of war or "lean cows that devour fat cows", in the dream of Pharaoh, interpreted by Joseph.

The profits generated by economic activity and especially the sale of minerals have been swallowed up in the purchase of weapons of mass destruction that have not been used.

Appendix

Expression of interest

' XiJi ' plan for Africa

TDR project fresh water

EXPRESSION OF INTEREST,

Call for contribution and Call for projects

I. Strategic objective of aimed sustainable development:

The African Union looks for partners for the implementation of the projects this - above enumerated to answer the stakes in the sustainable development and in the emergence in 2025.

II. The stakes and the challenges in order of priority

Priority or Stake N°1:

The African Union says that the urgency and the absolute priority of Africa is;
The production of fresh water, by desalination of sea water, and its transport to the dry lands of Africa, in particular the sahelo-Sahelian zone will remain the basic project (urgent and priority), with big capital gains for all Africa

For Central Africa
- From Kribi to the Lake Chad, from N'Gaoundéré to Juba (the South Sudan), a plan of the water, adjoining, to the network pipeline transporting the crude oil of DOHA to Kirby.

A refilling, in small daily dose, of the Lake Chad, until its level of former days.

The dry lands of the South of the Chad, the North Cameroon, the North of the Centrafrique will be made cultivable, in fruits and vegetables, by the presence of the fresh water

- From Lobito to the dry lands of the South of Angola

For western Africa;
- From Nouadhibou to Kidal, to Timbuktoo and to Agadez
- From Nouakchott to Mopti, where the river NIGER will be refilling in fresh water, in small daily doses.
- From Saint-Louis to Kayes, where the Senegal River will be refilling fresh water, in small daily doses
- From Kaolack to Kédougou / Saraya, to cultivate all of the lands of Senegal
- From Ziguinchor (to cultivate all of the lands of Casamance) to Sikasso where Djoliba will be refilling in fresh water, in small daily doses
- From San Pedro to Bobo Dioulasso, by watering the lands of the north of Ivory Coast and the South of Burkina Faso (From Taboo to Taï, samatiguila then Manankoro, from Grand Lahou to Daloa then Korhogo then to Ouangolodougou,)
- From Newtown to Kotouba then to Gaoua and in OUAGADOUGOU)
- From Cotonou, to Malanville, to Tillabéry to Agadez, watering the lands of the South of Niger. The river NIGER will be refilled in fresh water, in small daily doses to Tillable.

- From BODOGRI, Shaky, Kalama, Koko, Tambawell, Sokoto) is going to anchor definitively NIGERIA in the project, with its diversion, Sokoto - Dosso-Niamey, Dosso-Zinder - Diffa and SOKOTO - Kitsna - Maiduguri-Lac Tchad

For east Africa
- From Djibouti (and Somalia land) to Ethiopia (and Eritrea to Sudan), to cultivate all of lands from the east of Africa where the famine and the drought rage regularly
- From Mombasa, to the lands of the North Kenya, the South Sudan
- From Maputo to Matébélé land, to spray the dry lands of Zimbabwe

For Egypt
From Alexandria, by irrigating drip along and across, the lands of the desert to the southern border, where the Nile will be fed, at sneaky small doses

For Libya's sake
From Benghazi to Lybia's desert lands, Chadian Tibesti Toubous lands and the borders of Agadez (NIGER)

For Southern Africa
- from Wallis bey to Malawi and Botswana and the Kalahari Desert
- Durban, to the arid lands of Lesotho and northern Republic of South Africa

For Madagascar
- from Toamasina to Ambrositra,
- from Mananjary to IHOSY
- from ANDROKA to BFTSIOKY
- TSARATANANA) and North East (BEFANDRIANA)

A perennial debt over 50 years to alleviate the effects of the Freshwater War and reduce poverty by increasing the irrigated perimeters and consequently the production of fruits and vegetables.
The sale of water will repay the loan through a private management company

In single project to take out all Africa of the famine, the poverty, of massive import of the absolutely essential food and eternal assistance.

The second urgency is the collection, the treatment (processing) and the recycling of urban waste

We are in the presence of a public health problem. It is enough to dolly (browse) our big cities to convince oneself. From then on, we are not surprised with the epidemic of cholera or of typhoid in Kinshasa or the proliferation of rats (of cemetery) in Brazzaville, and in Lagos.

Construction of urban waste processing factories in all the big cities of Africa.

The ' waste urban ' tax will be taken from every household (housework) or citizen to make this ecological activity profitable, to make them managed by young people in companies.

Stake N°3:

The permanent availability of electricity everywhere in the continent as one of the conditions of the emergence, on the horizon 2025

The African Union, in the achievement of its objectives of realizing conditions bringing to the emergence of Africa, has retained as the third condition and priority, the plentiful and cheap production of the squeaky clean appropriate and ecological electricity, through:
- The construction of all the hydroelectric dams,
- The valuation of the GNL by the construction of gas plants
- The setting-up of power plants with renewable energies and
- The implementation of the meshing HV/THT of the whole continent

The renewable energies, including the hydroelectric, remain the simple and fast solution of a accelerated and harmonious development, which bases itself on a clean and long-lasting source of energy AD AETERNAM

The valuation of the Gas, wiped on platforms and in reserve.
This project consists in liquefying the gas, at present wiped and in reserve underground, in storing it in large quantities then to:
- Export. There will be built by methane ports as well as storage areas with big capacity to facilitate the storage and the export of the liquefied gas. The studies will also deal with the possible purchase contracts of the gas as the mode of guarantee of the investments.
- Consume locally in the continent. The industries of bottling of the domestic and industrial gas, will be set up and the conditions of distribution and low cost selling will be formalized. These industries will be sold to private ones to guarantee the loan but also to bring to the foreground the economy by the diversification.

Stake N°4:

Implementation, in the regions of extraction of ores, industries Of Refining of ores (iron, copper, aluminum, oil ...)
It is about initializing on the neighboring sites the deposit, the processing procedure of ores.
From iron ore to steel locally: Gabon and Congo could together acquire blast furnaces, rolling mills and steel mills to refine on

site 15 to 25% of the ore mined, within a five-year horizon, and reach 50 % in 2025.

These industries will include blast furnaces and rolling mills necessary for the treatment of iron minerals Extracts of the deposit of Mayoko and the production of the steel.

Zambia wishes to carry in 50 %, its capacity of the refined copper locally production
RD Congo will be supported to equip itself with materials and transformation equipment of the copper to Lubumbashi.

The bauxite, of Cameroon and Guinea Conakry, will be by the abundant and cheap electricity, refined in 90/95 %.

The installation of steel-based industries, including assembly lines of all types (cars, locomotives, wagons, trains, etc.)

The project has for object to install durably the iron and steel-based industries for the local production of every typical chap of material and machines, from the cheap steel of Congo and Gabon and from the copper of Zambia and DR Congo

The space agency FUNSU ZINGA will be the ultimate objective of the steel-based industries, for the lowest costs in the world, due to the presence of a very cheap electricity
Africa enters the spatial era

Stake N°5

The knowledge economy and the digital economy or the construction of:
- Two to ten university centers by Country
- Universities dedicated to the sustainable development for the countries of the lays of Congo.
- A building, by department, sheltering the center of incubation of the companies of the young entrepreneurs and START - Up

The African Union decided to work on the fiber optic Project in Africa:
- Bring the fiber optic in all the African countries
- To cable all the cities of Africa with high broadband, 10 - 100 Mbits/s

Stake N°6:

The construction of the single sky and the opening of the air transport market in Africa

- Serving President of the African Union, on 2019, will lead the meeting of all the aviation service providers of the continent, which will end in the agreements of the ANS PROVIDERS project of interconnection and interoperability

- The meeting will be pronounced on the project of the secondary aerodromes of all the countries of Africa, to fill the gap, the holes of the blanket of flight safety and the lack of skills of the DACs
- The project in the African single sky satellite of aeronautical telecommunications will be discussed and validated to serve as a solid foundation of the African single sky

In 2019, / 2020 serving president, will gather the experts to take the lead in the transportation market in Africa on the following projects:

Project "poles of leasing of planes"

Project "centers of maintenance of planes, certified"

Project "modification of the legislation of countries for the validation of the air transport market"

Project "fund of financing of the leasing of planes"

Project "insurances of planes on the continent"

Stake N°7

The layout of the new lines, the construction of electrical tracks and stations are the main focus of this project. The new lines are:

- ➤ North West line, 3,600 km; Kinshasa / Bandundu / Lisala / Gbadolité / Zongo
- ➤ North East line, 4,000 km; Kinshasa / Bokungu / Kisangani, Bonalia, Buta, Juba

- ➤ East line, 3,500 km; Kinshasa / Kananga / Kindu / Bukavu / Goma / Kigali
- ➤ South line, 3,500 km; Kinshasa / Kenge / Kikwit: Tchikapa / Kamina / Lubumbashi
- ➤ West line, 600 km ; Kinshasa / Brazzaville / Pointe Noire, via the road bridge rails
- ➤ Southwest line, 1,500 km; Kinshasa / Luanda
- ➤ Other lines: Katanga / Kassaï / Benguela

Stake N°8

Taken together, the second wealth of Central African countries (ECCAS) will be the ability to conserve intact forest ecosystems for future generations.
The goal is to accept the conservation of forests as the wealth of tomorrow

The momentum of forest conservation, Congo Basin ecosystems and the environment will lead us to reduce (15% per year and for five successive years) the cutting of trees. Wood will be taken less and less in forests, up to 75% by 2025, for the sake of our traditional pharmacopoeia and for the sake of future generations

The momentum of forest conservation, Congo Basin ecosystems and the environment will lead us to reduce (15% per year and for five successive years) the cutting of trees. Less and less wood will be taken from forests, up to 75% at the end of the year. their cars / vehicles fossil fueled by new models environment-friendly and of the climate.Proposals of assembly lines are waited.

III. Conditions of the implementation of these projects and deadline of receipt:

Besides the usual facilitations of the code of investment, the present projects. The offers of studies, financing and partnership are received, immediately, in the office of the African Union.

Serving President of the African Union

A "XiJi" plan for Africa in a privileged partnership with the ZLEC of all Africa

A "XiJi" plan for Africa in the framework of the privileged partnership between China and Africa, with the Free Trade Zone - ZLEC

Like the MARSHALL plan, which made it possible to rebuild Europe after the two wars, the "XiJi" plan will accelerate the sustainable development of Africa in the five axes chosen by the privileged partnership.

The September forum in Beijing will make it possible to launch this plan

Topics	Action	Evidence and amounts
Fresh water	Install seawater desalination plants 5 units of 200 000m3, per site 20 sites (Nouadhibou, Nouakchott, Saint Louis, Kaolack, Ziguinchor,...) Transport water from the sea to the arid lands of the interior of the continent Sell fresh water to repay the loan To be able to plant vegetables and fruit trees quantitatively for food security Put fruits and vegetables into long-term storage by agri-food industries	Fight famine, drought, poverty, and water wars in Africa. 94 billion euros to be mobilized for all Africa in a 50-year long-term debt
Urban waste	Install city waste collection, treatment and recycling centers, dumped into rivers	A private business to be profitable

	and oceans	through the sale of recycled products and citizen contributions of $ 1 per quarter and per individual
Electric energy	Electricity generation, ecological, abundant and cheap Hydroelectric dams (Inga III, Kouilou Sounda, Kasai I & II) Laying tidal turbines, on both banks, 4000 km from the river CONGO Electricity generation, by LNG, through the extinction of flares on oil platforms; 3 to 5 GW per crude producing country Installation of HV / HVT transmission / distribution / sale lines throughout Africa	30 billions euros Profitability through the sale of electricity by PPA, payable in advance, through a financial package where there will be no arrears to recover

Topics	Actions	Evidence and amounts
Refining ores locally before export	Installation of blast furnaces, steel mills and rolling mills in the region between Owendo (Gabon) and Mayoko (Congo), near the ore extraction site	Local production to assist in the establishment of steel-based industries
The rail network is to be built	First, to link the Malébo Pool (Brazzaville and Kinshasa) to all the ECCAS capitals (Libreville, Brazzaville, Bangui, N'Djamena, Juba, Kigali, Bujumbura, Lusaka, Luanda); 50 to 100 000 km of railways to lay, Second : connect Dakar to Addis Abeba, serving Bamako Passage, Ouagadougou, Niamey, Diffa, Maiduguri, N'Djamena, Juba. branch lines on Ziguinchor, Bissau, Conakry, Abidjan, Lomé, Cotonou, Lagos	At first, locomotives, wagons and rails will come from China In a second step, it will be envisaged their manufacture on the continent, in particular between the Congo and Gabon, because of the iron ore and the rolling mills / steelworks which will be installed not far from the extraction

		sites
		Low-cost, locally produced green electricity would provide the lowest production costs in the world.
The all electric in the transport in Africa, trains, cars, boats, taxis and drone	The introduction of cars and electric trains, as of 2020, in the CFTA is an economic asset and a stake in the fight against air pollution. Chinese manufacturers could introduce the Renault Zoe, under license, and after developing their own model, cost ex factory of 5,000 / 6,000 euros, after organizing the distribution network of spare parts, the collection of used batteries and the installation of multi-source charging stations in the continent. The third generation of cars	Replacement of fossil-fueled models by all-electric and hydrogen models

	will be manufactured locally as a result of the refining of minerals and the abundance of cheap electricity	
	The taxicab drones will have their places, after the statement of the laws and regulations of their use as aircraft by the civil aviation	
	Under-equipped Africa will easily dispose of its fossil-fueled models if the privileged partnership seizes the opportunity	
The civil aviation business in the ZLEC	If China has ordered 150 Airbus for its own needs, it can acquire 100 additional Airbuses and exploit the internal market of Africa Thus, a maintenance workshop will be established on the continent for this purpose It will be able to take over the management of the continent's airport concession by providing new passenger control equipment	Africa is an opportunity with the opening of the air transport market and the construction of the unique African sky

	(airport interconnection and real-time "border crossing" data exchange). The launch of a satellite would merge the ANS PROVIDERS of the continent and halve the aeronautical fees	
The knowledge and digital economy	Over 5 successive years, China will have to train a minimum of 55,000 African students, or 1,000 per country, to make up for Africa's increasing technical deficit in all specialties. An effort will be made to build 5 to 10 university centers per country, in order to set the youth on their resort site The emblematic university hubs such as the school of all branches of meteorology or the university of forest ecosystem conservation sciences and trades will be given priority	Knowledge and technology transfer can be combined with ecology

	All cities in Africa will be provided with fiber optic cable and the refund will be guaranteed by private management	
Conservation of forest ecosystems	The presence of water will reforest all savannahs and drylands Only planted trees will be cut for the needs of the industry Natural forest trees will be closed to logging for the conservation of forest ecosystems By copying on CANADA and with the help of China, we can grow sea fish, aquaculture, along the coast, the continent Re-seeding laboratories for over-consumption species will be set up to help raise sea and freshwater fish	From today, and urgently, we must clean the planet, recycle our urban and toxic waste and finally reseed the seas and forests with over-consumption species

TDR freshwater

Terms of reference

FRESHWATER TRANSPORT PROJECT,
FROM KRIBI TO LAKE CHAD,
From N'Gaoundéré to JUBA, via BRIA (North RCA)

TRANSPORT OF FRESHWATER FROM KRIBI TO LAKE CHAD, N'Gaoundéré to JUBA, via BRIA*

The route of freshwater transport from Kribi to Lake Chad will be adjacent to Chad's oil pipeline from Doha to Kribi

SUMMARY

1. CONTEXT OF STUDY (Proposed Projects)

2. OBJECTIVES COVERED

3. EXPECTED RESULTS

4. QUESTIONS TO STUDY

5. REPORTS AND DELIVERABLES

6. TIMING

7. SUMMARY OF TDRS

1. CONTEXT OF THE STUDY (proposed projects)

The AU, through ECCAS / CEMAC, plans to focus on improving transport conditions, including the transport of fresh water from KRIBI to Lake Chad.

The present TERMS OF REFERENCES focus on the possibility of transporting fresh water from Kribi to the arid lands of Chad, North Cameroon, North RCA and South Sudan.

The sea level is rising and experts confirm a meter in the next ten years, mainly due to climate change.

The total area of the oceans is 360 700 000 km2 and that of the Atlantic Ocean is 106 100 000 km2. With 1 m of increasing level, it is estimated that the volume of water is 106,100,000,000 m3, or 106,100 Gm3.

The project plans to collect one million m3 of seawater per day through five units of 200,000 m3 each.
An annual consumption of 0.365 Gm3 of seawater that gives a quantitative assessment of the environmental impact on the , Atlantic Ocean.

The five units will desalt the seawater and produce us fresh water, at a rate of one million cubic meters per day.

Through a system of pipes and water towers, fresh water will be transported, mainly from KRIBI to Lake Chad, along a route passing from N'Gaoundéré, Garoua, Maroua and NDJAMENA.

Other routes are proposed to the authorities, to integrate the water needs of North Cameroon, North of NIGERIA and North of the Central African Republic.
The project recommends the creation of a private freshwater management company delivered, to guarantee the repayment of the loan and the quality of the product.

A related project, production of Fruits and Vegetables, is joined, begins with the planting, massively, in very great quantity, of the fruit trees, on all the irrigated perimeters made cultivable by the presence of the fresh water.

2. OBJECTIVES COVERED

Project title	Impact of the project	Remarks / Observations
The production of fresh water by the five seawater desalination plants, located around KRIBI, along the Atlantic coast, with a daily capacity of 200 000 m3, each one million m3	Availability of fresh water in all the arid zones of the four countries mentioned Increase by irrigation, drip, cultivated perimeters (1000 km x 1000 km) Increase in the production capacity of fruits and vegetables, following the planting of fruit trees Possibility of packaging fruits in juice and vegetables in long-term storage.	Each factory costs 40 billion FCFA, or 200 billion for the five units and with 1 billion for distribution pipes around each city crossed, creating more than 5 million km2 of irrigated perimeters The main stretch of Kribi, N'Gaoundere, Garoua, Maroua, N'Djamena and Lake Chad is estimated at 400 billion

Project title	Impact of the project	Remarks / Observations
Mesh, of each city of the route (N'Gaoundéré, Garoua, Maroua, N'Djamena, Moundou, Sarh), by portion 50 km x 50 km, by pipes of distribution of fresh water on the whole of the arid zones of the four countries ; Chad, CAR, Nigeria, and Cameroon	Expected agribusiness boom will improve the purchasing power of farmers and industrial farmers Further socialization of nationals across all irrigated areas A leading role in agricultural production in the Central Africa subregion	Sales of 1,000,000 m3 at 100 F per m3, or 100 million F per day, or 2.4 billion FCFA per month, or nearly 30 billion per year One can repay, by selling water through a private freshwater management company The cost of the m3, imposes the education and the sensitization of the peasants, with the mode of watering drip

The main route starts from Kribi, crosses the cities (N'Gaoundéré, Garoua, Maroua) and ends in Lake Chad, where it will replenish the lake, in small doses, in fresh water.

The route of the freshwater transport, which is next to that of Chad's oil pipeline, from Kribi to N'Gaoundéré, before marrying the diversions
- From N'Gaoundéré, Garoua, Maroua to Lake Chad, via N'Djamena
- From Maroua to Maiduguri
- From N'Gaoundéré, to Moundou, SARH, GONDEY, BIRAO, AMDAFOK
- From N'Gaoundéré, Gouza, Kaga bandara, Bria, Yalinga, Bougou to Juba

3. EXPECTED RESULTS

- At the end of the main route, Lake Chad, will be refueled, in small daily doses until it reaches its level of yesteryear

- Creation of a PRIVATE COMPANY FOR THE MANAGEMENT OF PRODUCTION, DRINKING WATER TRANSPORT
A private company will be created to manage the freshwater production infrastructure, with desalination plants of seawater, for various reasons

1. Guarantees

The potability of the verified water and its guaranteed quality, according to the international standards in the matter, will be the first requirements of private management of this fresh water.

Water sold by Water Purchase Agreement (WPA) to wholesalers that are NATIONAL WATER DISTRIBUTION COMPANIES and / or any private licensed in the distribution or sale of water, is payable in advance at the beginning of each month by the beneficiary's bank. No arrears to recover

2. The financial package

Borrowing	The variants	Observations
Bond borrowing from public markets and private savings in CEMAC and economic zones (CEEAC)	Contribution of concerned states (through the Congo Basin Blue Fund), 20% BDEAC, 40% ADB, 40%	Loan amount 1 500 billions Duration of loan 50 years Annuity 30 billion Interest rate 7%

3. The distribution of the shares of the company producing freshwater

States concerned	International financial and private organizations	Share reserved for national private citizens of the four states and CEMAC / CEEAC zones
20 %	60 %	20 %

- THE PRODUCTION OF FRUIT AND VEGETABLES AND AGRI-FOOD COMPANIES

The presence of fresh water will transform arid lands (North Cameroon, North Nigeria, North Central Africa and South Chad) into irrigated perimeters and arable land.

It will then be possible to plant fruit trees over an area of nearly 1000 km by 1500 km, and manage this abundant fruit and vegetable production, in any season, through a fruit and vegetable company in Central Africa (SOFRUILAC).

A large planting / seed distribution campaign will be undertaken with the farmers who benefit from the irrigated perimeters, to support and assist them in the agricultural activity, until the purchase of all their production (Fruit and Vegetable Purchase Approval) by the farmers. agri-food units.

The agribusinesses who will be in charge of transforming / conditioning a large part of this production of fruits and vegetables, will find considerable gains.

- AQUACULTURE AT LAKE CHAD

One objective of the project is to replenish Lake Chad, in small doses per day in fresh water.
It is possible to reach in two years, a quarter of the maximum level of the lake and thus to validate the aspect AQUACULTURE with the lake, with its laboratory of breeding and seeding, for a quantitative production of all the species of fish.

Residents will be trained / assisted by sustainable development specialists.

Minimal fees for "right to fish" will be collected to compensate for the water supply from Lake Chad. Participatory citizen solidarity

4. QUESTIONS TO STUDY

Estimated cost of the project

Rubric	Estimate
5 Seawater desalination plants	240 billions
Transport pipes, pipeline, freshwater	1200 billions
Water distribution pipe networks for the creation of irrigated perimeters	12 billions
Assisted fruit tree planting Training support and credit access to farmers	3 billions
Amount	1 500 billions

Estimated income (estimate of the revenues)

Daily Production	Annual Production	Unit cost of m^3	Annual revenue
200,000 m^3 x 5 units is 1,000,000 m3 per day	365 000 000 m^3	100 FCFA	36,5 billions FCFA

Blocking factors are:

- the duration of the loan will be negotiated "perennial", 50 years

- the water will be sold under Water Purchase Agreement, and paid in advance, at the beginning of each quarter by the wholesaler's bank and the peasant and village cooperatives. No debt and no money to recover.

5. REPORTS AND DELIVERABLES

The consultants will submit a final report within 25 weeks after the date of the Call for Projects and Expression of Interest.

The final report will provide the results and conclusions of the evaluation. It will not contain more than 20 pages and appendices, will be in French and must be submitted by .... [date] at the latest.

6. TIMING

T0	T1	T2	T3	T4
Official launch date of the project and Call for expressions of interest, and Call for projects	+ 3 months Selection of projects received, notificatio n	+1 month APS, delivered, Restitutio n meetings, Collection of correction s	+1 month APD, DCE, DAO delivered, Restitutio n meetings, Collection of correction s	+1 month final deliverabl es, AOR Launch, Project Selection, Adjudicati on

7. SUMMARY OF TDRs

The projects listed above absorb much of the shortcomings and shortcomings in the production and transport of freshwater in the arid lands of the interior of the continent.
The projects received will be selected and awarded, by mutual agreement, after negotiation of the price schedule.
The present TDRs, the call for projects and the notice of expression of interest are worth a Restricted Invitation to Tender (AOR), given the nature of the skills requested before the selection.

The current President of the African Union

Dedications

To the souls who aspire to join us, in this effort to awaken this Africa, not only the cradle, but also, and above all, the near future and desirable future of Humanity !

To Paul Kagame, who has managed to defeat the shadow that every man has in him, to give this strategy, of all Africa in a single free trade zone, in 2018, in his capacity as President in office of the African Union.

To Anatole Bizongo, who brought me, on a trip to Kinshasa at his own expense, to take a fresh look at the place and role of this giant, which is DR Congo, in Central Africa.

To Andréa Malewa, who tries to wake up, those on the right bank of the Congo River, paralyzed by the long bite of Marxist-Leninist and racist incivism, which has already engendered predators. He commands the respect, even of his political opponents, under the bewildered fear of his compatriots, before so much courage and daring. Another Congo is possible!

A Junior, 3M-A, Maungu Minguiel Michelangelo, the "Mu kongo", in order to consolidate the argumentation of the Global Change to "build the nucleus", the "n'zita dia nza", the driving torque of the Central Africa).

To Patricia J N, your eyes were my best mirror, that was yesterday!

ACRONYMS

AZAWAD, is a territory almost entirely desert located in the North of Mali

ICAO, International Civil Aviation Organization

AU, African Union

CEMAC, Economic and Monetary Community of Central Africa

ECCAS, Economic Community of Central African States

DRC, Democratic Republic of Congo

RC, Republic of Congo

DACs, Civil Aviation Directorate

TDRs, Terms of Reference

Bibliography and data source

A / Books

Verona Manckou, 2014, "CONGO : Terre des technologies Objectif 2025", Harmattan

Pierre Jacquemot, 2016, "Africa of possibilities: The challenges of emergence", Karthala edition

Jean Emmanuel Pondi, 2015, "Thomas Sankara and the emergence of Africa in the 21st century", Africa edition Awakening

Walter Rodney, 1972, "How Europe Underdeveloped Africa: A Historical Analysis of Underdevelopment", Caribean editions

Jacques Brasseur, 2016, "Economic History of Tropical Africa, From Origins to Today", Armand Colin Edition

1 In HUGO, "Introduction to the history of contemporary Africa", Editions Armand Colin, Paris, 1998

2. Arlette and R RUCHELLI, "Lexicon of the social sciences", Paris, Moder company, 1996

3. BAGENDA, "Congo sick of its men", editions Luc Pire, Brussels, March 2003.

4. B.ADAM, "The reality of arms transfers", Paris, December 1996.

5. Eddie Tambwe Kitenge Kitoko Bin, "DR Congo : the elections and after" Intellectuals and politics pose the stakes of the post-transition, "Harmattan edition, 2006.

6. St. Louis University Faculties, "What Future for Environmental Law?" Brussels, 1996.

7. P.M.MATUMBA NGOMA, " The DRC: a democratization at the end of the rifle", Kinshasa, Fondation KONRAD ADENAUER Editions. 2006

8 GRIP, "Conflicts in Africa, Crisis Analysis and Pathways for Prevention", Complexe Edition, Brussels, 1997.

9. GRIP, " Media and conflict, vector of war or peace actors ", Complexe Edition.

10. J-Y. LOVOIE, " The foreign question of the development of Africa", Presses de l'université Québec, 1986

11. Mr GRAWITTZ, "Methods in Social Sciences", Dalloz Publishing, Paris, 2001.

12. M.-F. CROSS and F. MISSER, "Geopolitics of Congo (DRC)", Complexe editions, 2006.

13. "Missionaries of Africa, Democratic Republic of Congo 2000-2001", document, Bukavu.

14. P. BAKENDA, "Congo sick of its men", LUCPIRE editions, Brussels, March 2003.

15. P. RICHARD, "What are these weapons for?", Éditions l'Épiphanie, Kinshasa, 1998.

16. P. BARACYETSE, "The Geopolitical Challenge of International Mining Companies in the DRC", SOS Rwanda Burundi, Belgium, 1998.

17. R. PINTO and M. GRAWITTZ, "Method of social sciences", 4th edition, Dalloz, Paris, 2011

18. R. MINANI BIHUZO, "Current Issues of Civil Society in the DRC and Perspective of Cooperation", Ed. CEPAS, Kinshasa, 2003.

19. R. DUMON, "The forest as a source of energy and new activity", 2nd edition, Masson, Paris, 1998, p.1.

20. E. NGOMBET, "Economic Intelligence in African Countries", 2018 Edilivre

B / DICTIONARY AND ENCYCLOPEDIANS

1. C. DOCTE, "Grand dictionary encyclopedia" Larousse, complete edition, vol3, Canada, 1982

2. "Dictionary of French", Larousse, May 2006

3. J-M. COLOMBANI, "Dictionary of economy" Larousse, 2000

C / ARTICLES, REVIEWS AND NEWSPAPERS

1. "The sustainable management of Congolese forests by indigenous people in the face of climate change", in Le forestier, n ° 4, December 2008

2. "Analysis of the socio-economic consequences of the Bukavu war", in UNDP, September 2004-June 2005.

3. "European Community, Environment and Development", in The Courier, Africa-Caribbean-Pacific, No. 133, May-June, 1992

4. "The Congolese woman: victim of violence, peacemaker", in MONUC Contents

5. Mr. EKWA BIS ISAL, "And our minerals were used to develop our agriculture and education system" in Renaissance, No. 02/03, 2011.

6. "The World Heritage", in The UNESCO Mail, September 1997.

7. "Conflict and war in Kivu and the Great Lakes region. Entre les tensions locales et escalade", in Institut Africain-CEDAF, N°33-38, éditions l'Harmattan, Paris, 1999.

8. United Nations, "The Directory on Small Arms", GRIP, 2001.

Table of contents

FROM THE SAME AUTHOR

- **Economic intelligence in African countries**
Edilivre 2018

- **France, plural and mixed race, world champion**
Edilivre 2018